Built on the principles that there is a place in this world for [illegible] all living things have feelings, and that all life has purpose, we [illegible] present the American Quarter Horse as a new "self-sacrificing, strong-heart[illegible] national symbol at a time when our country is at risk. Inspirationally, educationally, and motivationally, *Tuffy, A Real American Quarter Horse Hero*™ , is one example of our citizenry taking responsibility for that which is right and acting upon it. Our goal is to facilitate character education and encourage the love of reading through creative writing. Tuffy, never perfect, but always focused, serves as a positive role model that works to overcome adversity and encourage others to succeed. In a country that struggles with cancer, depression, divorce, addiction, heart attacks and more we remain mindful that: "Perseverance produces character; and character, hope." Respectfully, we dedicate this book to all of the hardworking people on farms across these United States of America.

Perseverance produces character; and character, hope.

Tuffy, A Real American Quarter Horse Hero ™, "THE FIRST HORSE EVER ENROLLED IN SCHOOL"℠ is a self-funded, privately-owned character education initiative created for the purpose of working in partnership with the Santa Rosa County (Florida) Education Foundation to provide a three dimensional delivery system for character education concepts and to build fluency for developing readers. Revenues generated by Tuffy, LLC are subject to sales tax. Proceeds from the local sales are granted by Tuffy, LLC to support SREF's Teacher Grants Program. Tuffy, LLC reserves the right to partner outside of Santa Rosa County, Florida with other nonprofit organizations to develop revenue streams intended to support the goal of each new partnership. For more information, please visit **www.gotuffygo.com.**

On a cool spring morning at Blue Ribbon Farms
Out in the meadow, not far from the barn,
Helen, the horse, was bursting with pride
To have her new baby, right there by her side.
"Be proud my sweet Tuffy, and listen to me,
A Quarter Horse is known for his work quality."

**"I was born one spring morning on
Blue Ribbon Farms."**

"Mom, you called me Tuffy? Is that my real name?"
"It's what we all call you. It's called a nickname.
One day a neighbor was visiting the farm;
Mrs. Tammy, my owner, was impressed with his charm."
"Wow!" he exclaimed, "that horse looks real tough.
He's calm and quite gentle. He's made of good stuff."

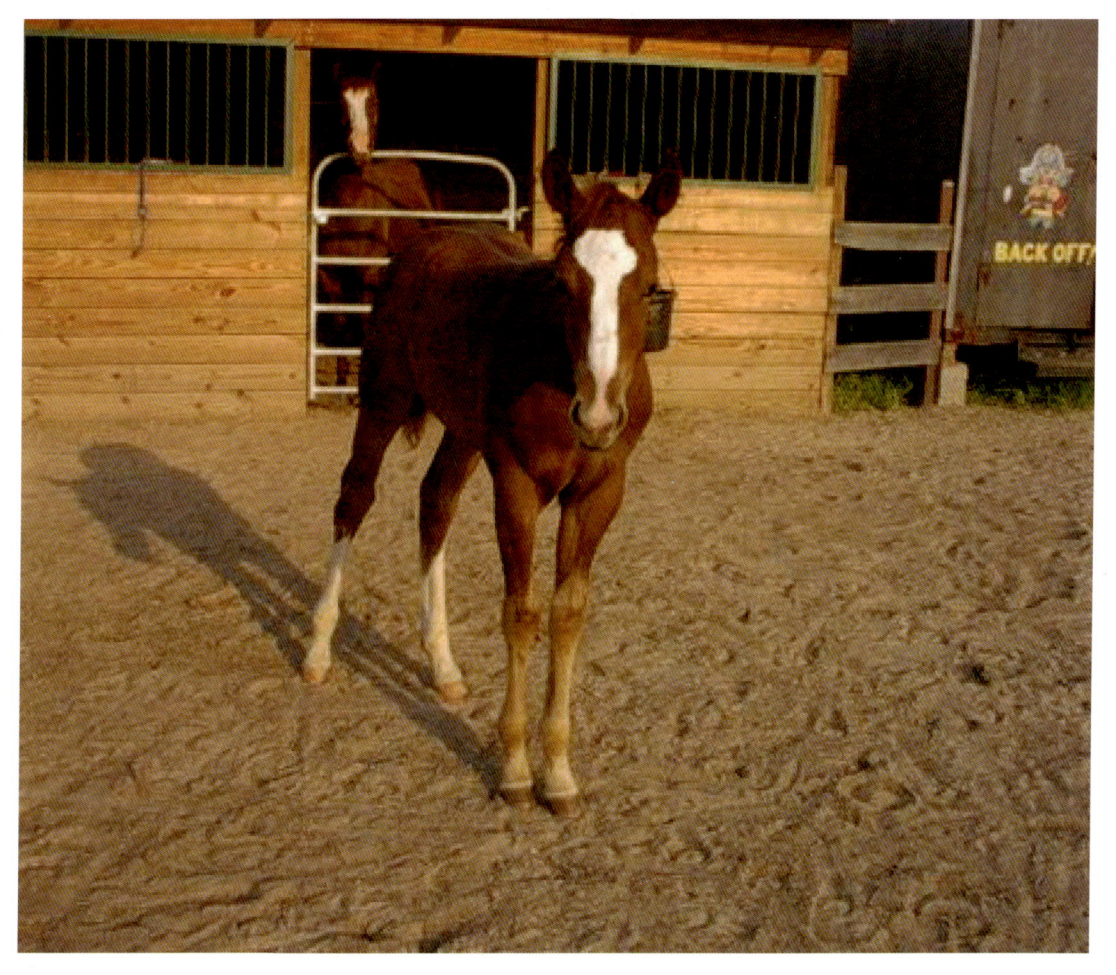

**"My nickname is Tuffy.
I am proud of my name."**

"So your nickname is Tuffy, but just so you know,
Your real name is Otoes Tough Man Go.
You're named for your father and your grandfather, too.
They're both special horses and quite proud of you."
"Where is my father, does he live far away?"
"On a farm in Alabama is where your dad stays."

"My birth certificate shows my family tree."

"Your grandpa worked harder than most horses do.
He was calf roping champ in 1972."
"I never met grandpa but I'm sure he would say,
'Never stop trying, despite what others say.
For success only happens when you give it your all.
It's not being perfect; you get up when you fall.'"

1ST IN THE NATION...

AQHA Champion Toebars, ridden by R. E. Josey, has been named Honor Roll Champion Calf Roping Horse of the nation by The American Quarter Horse Association.

During the 1972 show season AQHA Champion Toebars, son of Otoe, showed in seven states under 28 judges. He won 26 firsts under 25 different judges (winning the Texas State Fair, Louisiana State Fair, Mississippi State Fair and other prestigious shows). His 51 Honor Roll points are the second highest total in Quarter Horse history — he will stand the 1973 breeding at Willow Brook Farms — Fee $500.

"My Grandpa was a hard worker."

"My momma is special, Mrs. Tammy says so,
'Helen's strong and she's loyal with good self control.'
My momma's not perfect; she's blind in one eye.
Mrs. Tammy saw past that and gave her a try.
It's O.K. to be different, we all deserve love.
No one likes to be hurt or made fun of."

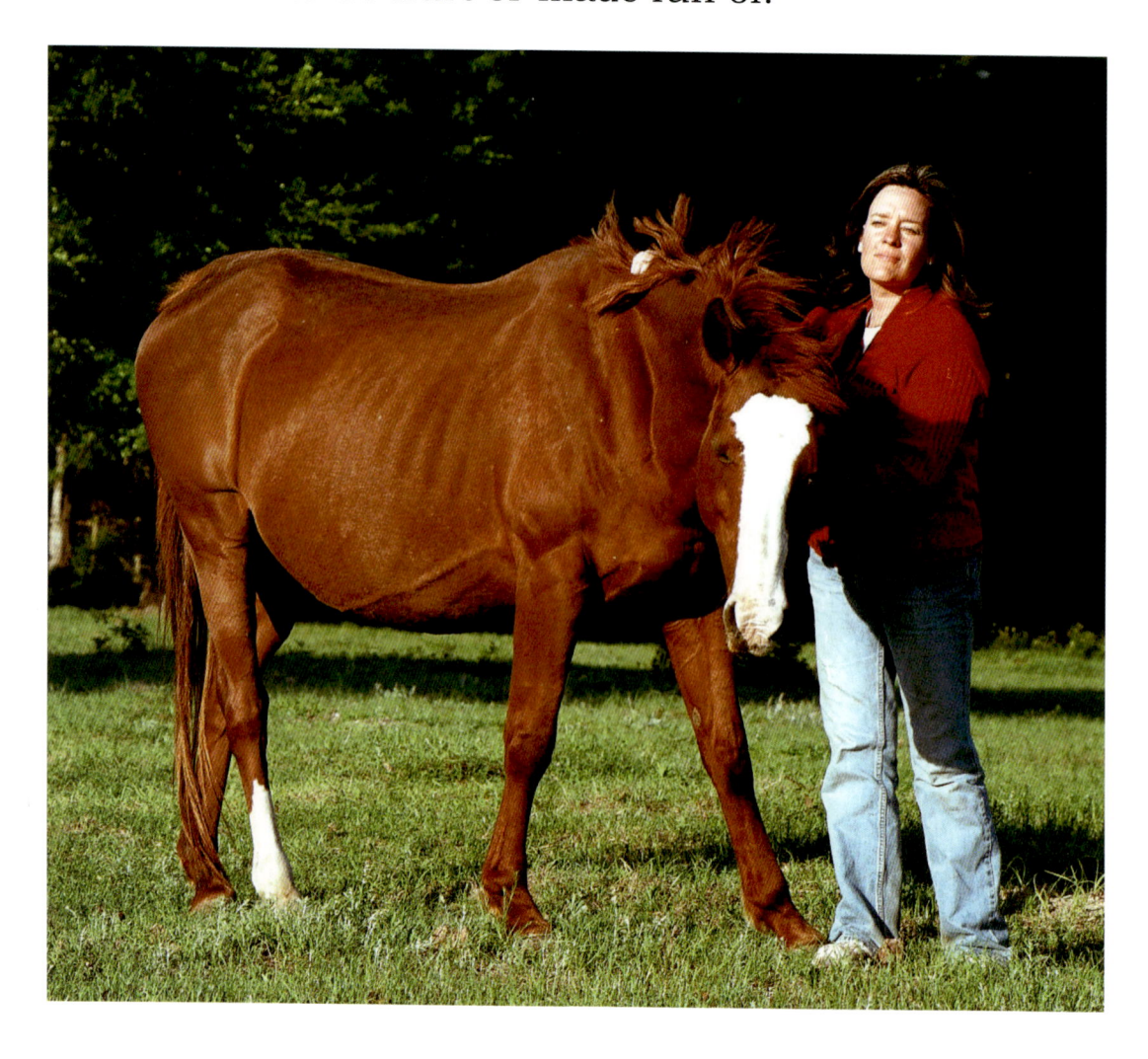

"My momma is special and loves me."

As Tuffy grew older he learned how to play.
His time with his mother grew shorter each day.
He ventured out farther, to see and explore,
To find what was out there, he had to know more.
Then one day his life changed, his future was set.
A man had a vision that had to be met.

Tuffy wants to know more about his world.

The new owner bought Tuffy because he believed
That Tuffy had potential to achieve and succeed.
"I'll put him in school and help him to learn
That success isn't given, it's something we earn."
The principal agreed and said with a smile,
"Let's get him enrolled, let him learn for a while."

Tuffy needed a classroom out on the range.

The desks were too small, Tuffy spoke words unknown.
"He's too big for this school. Why, he's almost full grown!"
His owner knew quickly, he needed a change.
He needed a classroom out on the range.
He knew of a place where a horse could be taught
The teacher, Mrs. Becky, said, "He must be brought!"

"I was too big for the bus and the school."

Soon Tuffy was transferred to Mrs. Becky's school.
He learned from her how to stay focused and cool.
"Tuffy, you need to stay calm; just relax.
We're all here to help keep you on the right track."
Whenever he's tired or the work is too tough,
He remembers his friends work hard when it's rough.

"I am learning to stay calm and relaxed."

When things are too hard, or he's just feeling shy,
Tuffy thinks of Dylan and how hard he tries.
Dylan is little; his legs are not long.
He works extra hard and he has to be strong.
He sets an example with the goodness he brings.
His small size won't stop him from doing big things.

"Dylan is my friend and always does his best."

Roper and Noel have taught Tuffy, too.
Two friends can do more work than just one can do.
When friends work together and do a job well
They work as a team, like Roper and Noel.
Friends can be helpful; two's better than one.
Having a friend can make all work more fun.

"My friends Roper and Noel work as a team."

Tuffy's friend Billy does his job every day.
He's stealthy and graceful and keeps mice away.
Billy works quietly, alone in the night.
You rarely will see him; he works out of sight.
"Billy is special; he's one of my friends."
Working together means everyone wins!

"While we are sleeping, Billy is hard at work."

Tuffy knows what it is to be a good friend;
How working together ties up the loose ends.
"I know I will have to be strong and believe,
When I've done all I can, I will always succeed.
My family and friends have all taught me well.
The lessons in life are the best stories to tell."

"My friends and I care for each other."

Character

When something is scary
Or too hard to do
When you really don't want
To do something that's new

Remember that someone else
Feels the same way
And the best thing to do
Is to try anyway

Just do your best
And your fears will be gone
And something that's new
Won't be new very long

Remember how Tuffy felt
Right at the start
And how he succeeded
By following his heart

For you are like Tuffy
You're big and you're brave
And when you succeed
It's a message that's saved

Reminding you always
How special you are
When you believe that you can
You will go very far.

© Tuffy, LLC 2007
Written by: Leslie Kaufmann
Photo by: Lynne Hough

Please accept our sincere appreciation and respect for making *Tuffy, A Real American Quarter Horse Hero*™ a real dream come true for us and for all the children we meet.
Special thanks to:
Teachers everywhere
Brad & Jan Prentice
Faculty, Staff, Administration and Students of East Milton Elementary School
Santa Rosa County School Board
Santa Rosa County Education Foundation
Mr. C.T. Fuller and Mr. Peter Fuller
Joe & Tammy Brown
Jeanne Pitts
AT&T Communications and Genie Nicholson
Paula Ward
Denise Blanchard
Cleta Miller
Lynne Hough
Brian Lewis
Patti Maddox
Cristin Axson
Phillip & Becky Hayes and Jill Hayes
Mark & Laura Staal
Mr. Arie Staal
The Spears Family of Trent's Prints & Publishing and AES Graphics
There are so many others who have made this project what it is and continue to push us to strive for more. To all of you, we sincerely thank you and appreciate your devotion and support. You are the ones who make this project successful and meaningful.

Special thanks to
Mr. R.E. and Martha Josey

In Memory of our Real Life Heroes

John C. Holley, Jr.
1931-1997

Robert L. Maddox, Sr.
1909-1976